CREEPY CHRONICLES

Haunted Homes

Written by Barbara Cox and Scott Forbes

Gareth Stevens
Publishing

CONTENTS

Are you afraid of the dark? Do ghosts give you a fright? Does even the thought of goblins, vampires, and monsters make your palms sweat and your skin tingle? Perfect...

You don't have to live in a haunted house or a spooky castle to be afraid (and fascinated) by the things that go bump in the night. The Bogeyman, mischievous poltergeists, terrifying phantoms, and menacing gargoyles are just some of the creepy things that make up our worst nightmares. But don't be scared! Everyone knows they're not real. Just make sure you sleep with one eye open.

HAUNTED HOMES

GHOST

GHOST

OTHER NAMES: Phantom, specter, wraith, spirit, spook, revenant, apparition.

FACT OR FICTION: Scientists say fiction, but many people would claim otherwise.

DESCRIPTION: Often a very pale, almost transparent version of the living person. Sometimes invisible. However, some ghosts look like ordinary people. Can be surrounded by extremely cold air. May shriek, sigh, or moan. Animals can also have ghosts.

WHERE THEY LIVE: Anywhere, such as old houses, castles, dark alleyways, theaters, stations, airfields, country roads, ruins, forests, and lakes.

POWERS: Can appear or disappear at will and may continue to haunt a place for hundreds of years, seeming indifferent to the passage of time. Can cause acute fear if they want to.

WEAKNESSES: Ghosts have a problem with salt—they don't like to cross it or touch it in any way.

DIET: Ghosts do not need to eat or drink.

OTHER CHARACTERISTICS: May be associated with a violent death, and appear every year on the anniversary of the killing. Certain places seem to attract ghosts and are known for hauntings.

A GHOST can appear after a person has died. Many ghosts are not scary at all, others are quite terrifying, but they're all mysterious. Nobody knows why they appear. If someone was murdered or died horribly in some way, after death they might come back to wreak revenge.

THE APPEARANCE OF GHOSTS

Phantoms, specters, and wraiths, which are the most frequently seen forms of ghosts, are pale grey or white in color, and misty. They seem to float in the air and you may be able to see right through them. Some ghosts can't be seen at all, but can only be felt as freezing cold air, especially if you walk through them! There may be a sense of dread, or just a feeling that someone is there.

The ghost of someone who was executed by beheading may walk around carrying his or her own severed head. A murder weapon may still be visible, such as a knife in their ghostly back. Other phantoms might display bloodied clothes or terrible wounds.

There are numerous stories of ghosts who appear to be a normal living person, until they suddenly disappear, walk through a closed door or solid wall, or perform some other supernatural act.

MYRTLES PLANTATION, LOUISIANA

Built in 1796, this house is said to be haunted by numerous ghosts. Supposedly, up to ten people have been murdered there, so it's not surprising. Ghosts of two little children have been seen playing on the veranda. Someone's last dying steps can be heard climbing the stairs. In one room where a soldier was killed, there is a body-sized blood stain which cannot be removed by any method. The ghosts of several slaves who met unfortunate deaths sometimes appear to ask if chores need doing. The grand piano plays by itself —just one haunting chord over and over again. One story claims that the spirits of a mother and her children are contained in a large mirror.

HAUNTINGS

If the ghost is someone who was murdered or died horribly, he or she is probably still angry about it. But sometimes they just seem to be fond of a particular place and decide to come back and haunt it.

Many ghosts seem to be stuck in a pattern that they have to repeat. For example, they always cross a certain room, look out of a particular window, or walk up a flight of stairs—sometimes the stairs are no longer there and the ghost climbs up in mid-air. These ghosts usually ignore people and may walk straight through them, which apparently feels rather strange if you're the person being walked through.

Other more malicious ghosts don't want to share their favorite place and walk around scaring off any living people who try to move in by terrorizing them with screams.

WARNING GHOSTS

Some ghosts are only seen when they show themselves in order to warn the living of a forthcoming event, usually a death in the family. Legend says that at Arundel Castle in Sussex, England, a white owl always appears when one of the family is going to die.

Other ghosts, more usefully, have been able to stop accidents, especially on train tracks, mountains, or roads—they appear at the place where they were killed themselves and warn the living to be more careful. These often look like ordinary people and witnesses may not realize there was anything strange about them until later.

ANIMALS AND GHOSTS

Ghosts of various animals have been seen, including those of dogs, cats, horses, deer, sheep, owls, and chickens. Living animals are also well known for being aware of ghosts. People first realize that there's a supernatural presence because their dog growls or snarls, apparently at thin air. Horses especially dislike ghosts, but cats seem to be less concerned.

There are tales of ghost hounds terrorizing travelers at night on lonely roads.

APPARITIONS

There are many cases of people having an unexpected vision of a relative, loved one, or friend, often someone who is far away, and then finding out later that the person died at exactly that moment. These ghosts usually seem very normal and are not distressed at all; they only appear once to give the news of their death and are not seen again. This kind of ghost may be called an apparition.

BERKELEY SQUARE

There is a terrifying ghost story attached to the address 50 Berkeley Square in London, England. The ghost of a madman is said to haunt the top bedroom of the house. If anyone spends the night in that room, it is said they will wake up either dead or insane.

GHOSTS IN FAMOUS PLACES

The Capitol Building in Washington, DC, is said to be haunted by several murdered politicians and two workmen who died while building its dome.

The ghost of Abraham Lincoln is said to haunt both the White House and Ford's Theater where he was assassinated.

The Château of Blois in France houses the ghost of a former Count of Blois. He fights against a ghostly enemy, in an endless duel, which has been going on since the sixteenth century.

Windsor Castle, home of the British royal family, has several royal ghosts, including Queen Elizabeth I and her mother Anne Boleyn, who runs down a long corridor while screaming.

The Tower of London, where the king's enemies used to be imprisoned before being put to death, is the most haunted building in Britain. The best known of its many ghosts is Margaret Pole, the Countess of Salisbury, who was executed in 1541 at age 71.

Top: The ghost of Queen Elizabeth I appears to England's Queen Victoria at Windsor Castle

COMMUNICATING WITH GHOSTS

A séance is a meeting of a group of people who try to get in touch with ghosts. They may use a ouija board, which is a board with the letters of the alphabet marked on it so that a ghost can spell out a message.

A medium is a living person who can communicate with the dead. In the nineteenth century, there was great interest in the afterlife, and people paid mediums large sums of money so that they could hear messages from their dead relatives or see a loved one's ghost.

A medium and her guests attempt to communicate with the dead.

GHOSTS AROUND THE WORLD

Ghosts are known in every country in the world and there are different customs for dealing with them.

Countries in Asia have a Ghost Festival, which may last as long as a month. This is a time when ghosts are free to roam the land of the living and must be looked after. In China, special attention is paid to hungry ghosts—the unhappy ones. It's important to make sure that these ghosts find their way back to Hell at the end of the festival.

The Day of the Dead in Mexico and other parts of Latin America is a time when people remember their dead relatives and friends and encourage them to come back and visit. Flowers are left for them and food is put out, on graves and in homes. The atmosphere is joyful, to welcome the ghosts, and motifs of skeletons and skulls are used as decorations.

Most of Europe has a tradition of remembering the dead on All Saints' Day and All Souls' Day (November 1 and 2), and in several countries a meal is left out and the house is kept warm for any ghosts who may visit at this time.

WHITE LADIES

There are many stories of pale ghostly women who haunt country roads or other remote places. They are usually the ghost of a local girl who was murdered, or had her heart broken and then committed suicide. Some White Ladies simply wail and moan, but many are angry at their fate and will try to lure passing men to their doom. Some haunt lonely bridges, such as the one in France who stops any man who tries to cross over and asks him to dance with her. If he refuses, she grabs him with terrifying strength and throws him down into the rushing river below.

Top left: The ghost of Okiku, a Japanese girl who was thrown down a well by her master for breaking a plate.
Left: Mexican decorated skull.

THE PHANTOM HITCH-HIKER — A MODERN WHITE LADY

On a deserted highway late at night, a solitary driver stopped to pick up a beautiful girl hitch-hiker. She sat quietly in the car and didn't say much. When they reached her destination, the driver looked around to see that she had vanished. Later, he learned that a girl died tragically near the same stretch of road.

Above and right: White Ladies are ghosts of broken-hearted women wishing to wreak revenge on living men.

POLTERGEIST

Above: Poltergeists are mischievous spirits that cause havoc in a house.

IF NO ONE CAN BE SEEN, but plates are thrown across the room, there's hammering on walls and floors in the middle of the night, and heavy furniture moves by itself, you might have a mischievous Poltergeist in your house.

MISCHIEVOUS SPIRIT

Unlike ghosts, which often show no interest in the people living in the house they are haunting, Poltergeists are definitely hostile to the human occupants. They break treasured objects, wait for them to be replaced, and then break them again.

Poltergeists continually make sudden loud noises so that nobody can relax. They especially like to stop human beings from sleeping, and may even bite, pinch, or hit them to keep them awake. Life with a Poltergeist soon becomes intolerable.

Often, when the exhausted family moves out, the Poltergeist disappears and will not trouble the next occupants at all. Families afflicted by a Poltergeist almost always include teenagers. Some believe that Poltergeists are drawn to the energy given off by a restless, and perhaps unhappy, child.

The Bogeyman is going to get you!

NIGHT MARE

A spirit that sits on your chest while you are asleep and gives you bad dreams.

In Scandinavia, the Night Mare is a female spirit called the Mara. She rides horses at night, leaving them mysteriously exhausted the next morning. In Germany, the Night Mare is male and is a kind of goblin called an Alp or a Trud. It gets in through the keyhole. In Japan, nightmares are brought by a monster called the Baku.

BOGEYMAN

The Bogeyman is a legend invented by parents to make small children behave.

The Bogeyman is a traditional scary figure which parents use to threaten their children, telling them that "the Bogeyman will get you if you leave the house alone/pick your nose/torture the pet cat" or whatever it may be. The Bogeyman is made as scary as possible by adults. Often he has long skinny arms for grabbing children, and he carries a sack on his back for taking the naughty ones away. The Bogeyman exists in every country and in every language.

YAKKA

An ugly Sri Lankan house demon which can cause disease and other troubles.

A Yakka is small, dark, and so incredibly hideous that you really don't want to look at it—meeting its gaze could make you very ill indeed. If you annoy a Yakka, it could even make you insane. Yakkas are believed to be the causes for almost all illnesses and misfortunes that happen around the home in Sri Lanka.

BOGGART

A nasty, hairy creature that lives in houses and can make people's lives miserable.

A Boggart is similar to a Poltergeist; it also likes to wreck houses, but there are some differences. A Boggart is usually visible, being described as short, hairy, and smelly. Moving will not solve anything if you have a Boggart—it always stays with the family it has decided to torture, so it will simply move with you.

Most Boggarts are found in the north of England, where they may live under a bridge while they wait for a new family to torment.

Hanging a horseshoe on the door of the house is said to keep Boggarts away.

CHANGELING

IF A CHILD wakes up one day and seems to have gone through a personality transformation, it might be a Changeling that has been left in place of the human child that was stolen by fairies during the night.

SUBSTITUTE CHILD

Sometimes, other beings—usually fairies, but also elves or trolls—decide to steal a human baby and bring it up themselves. They take the baby and leave another child in its place. This is called a Changeling.

Sometimes the Changeling is not even a fairy child, but a substitute made by magic out of a twig, in which case it will soon sicken and die. Changeling children that do survive are often strange-looking, difficult to manage, bad-tempered, and lacking in affection—though they are usually clever.

It seems fairies like to steal a human baby that is attractive to look at. In Ireland, it was once considered dangerous to compliment a mother loudly about how pretty her baby was, in case the fairies should hear.

Changelings will probably just leave their human family one day and go back to their own kind, but it's very unlikely that the human child will ever come back.

GARGOYLE

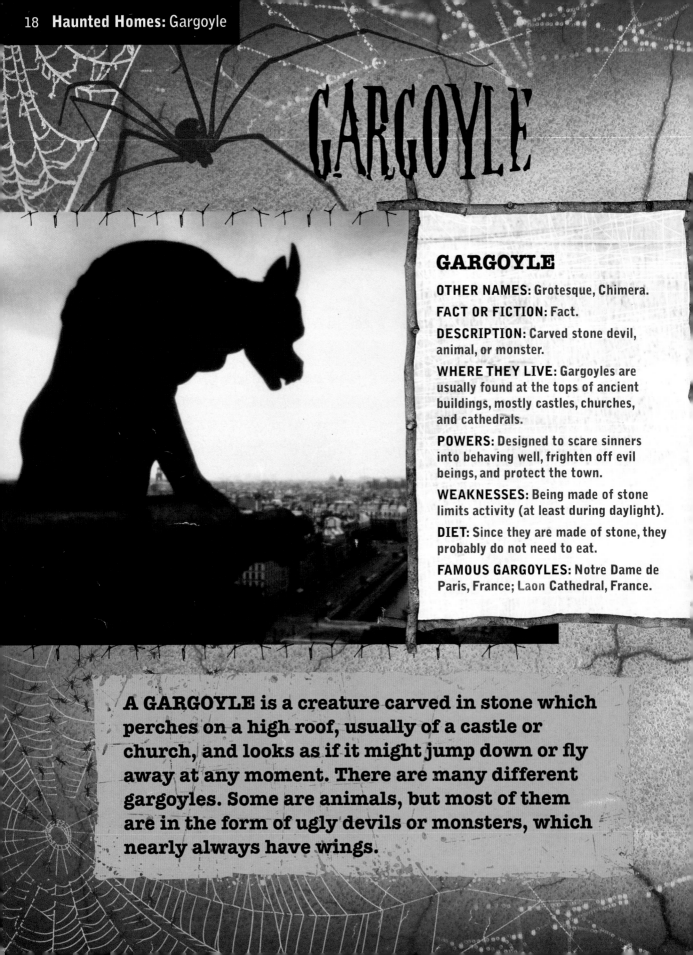

GARGOYLE

OTHER NAMES: Grotesque, Chimera.

FACT OR FICTION: Fact.

DESCRIPTION: Carved stone devil, animal, or monster.

WHERE THEY LIVE: Gargoyles are usually found at the tops of ancient buildings, mostly castles, churches, and cathedrals.

POWERS: Designed to scare sinners into behaving well, frighten off evil beings, and protect the town.

WEAKNESSES: Being made of stone limits activity (at least during daylight).

DIET: Since they are made of stone, they probably do not need to eat.

FAMOUS GARGOYLES: Notre Dame de Paris, France; Laon Cathedral, France.

A GARGOYLE is a creature carved in stone which perches on a high roof, usually of a castle or church, and looks as if it might jump down or fly away at any moment. There are many different gargoyles. Some are animals, but most of them are in the form of ugly devils or monsters, which nearly always have wings.

WATERSPOUTS BUT WHY SO SCARY?

The official explanation for gargoyles is that they were originally put on roofs to act as waterspouts. The word "gargoyle" is connected to "gurgle" and "gargle." The rainwater would run down the roof of the building into gutters and then through the gargoyles, which would act like fountains to project the water outward through their mouths and prevent it from soaking into the stone walls and damaging the building. But that doesn't explain why the gargoyles were made in the form of devils and monsters, or why many gargoyles actually aren't waterspouts at all, but just statues.

Many gargoyles are on churches and cathedrals, so the big mystery is: Why are such evil-looking creatures up there on the roof of a holy building? One theory is that they're intended to frighten people as they go in and out of the church to worship— showing them what evil things are waiting to punish them if they leave the protection of the church.

GUARD DEVILS

Another idea is that they're tame devils and are there to protect the building. In the same way as a guard dog would protect you against wolves, the gargoyles are there to guard the building against bigger and nastier devils who might come by. The fact that nobody's seen any of the bigger and nastier devils simply means the gargoyles are doing a good job. This would explain why they often seem to be watching out across the rooftops, rather than looking down at the people below. They're on the lookout for anything really bad that might fly past.

PROTECTING THE TOWN

In medieval times, the church was at the center of a town's society, and its gargoyles were seen to be protecting the whole town. Although they're trapped in stone during the day, some were believed to fly free at night and patrol the skies over the town, keeping everybody safe from any passing demons, unfriendly dragons, or other evil beings.

Although gargoyles are ugly and scary to look at, they're unlikely to harm you; although if you stand in the wrong place, they might spout water down onto your head. Some experts advise that gargoyles dislike being photographed, so it's better only to take photos of them when they're looking the other way.

Opposite and right: Gargoyles from Notre Dame Cathedral in Paris.

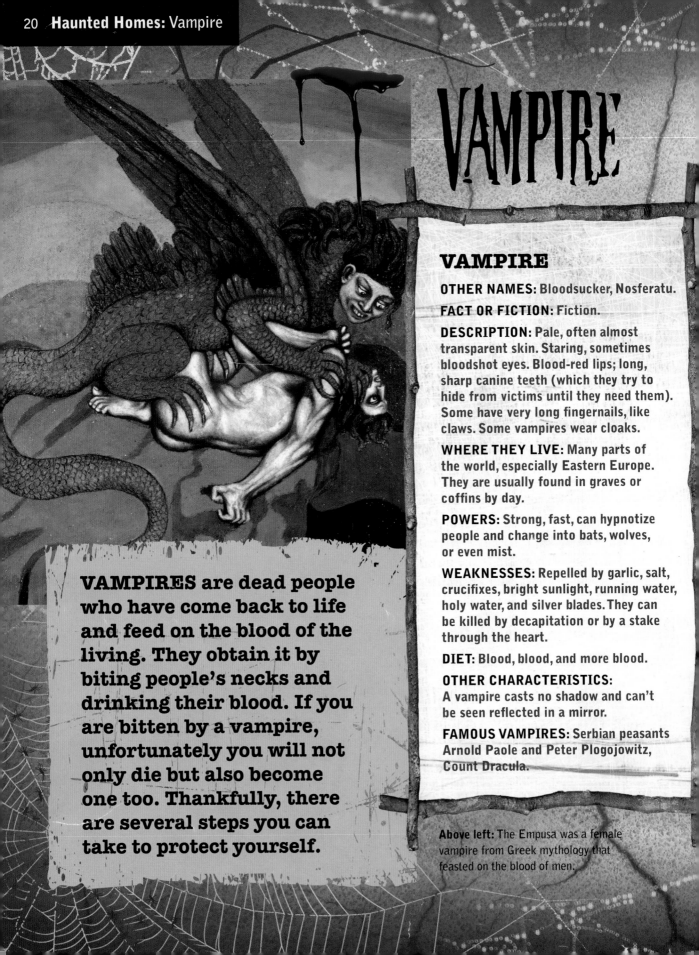

VAMPIRE

VAMPIRE

OTHER NAMES: Bloodsucker, Nosferatu.

FACT OR FICTION: Fiction.

DESCRIPTION: Pale, often almost transparent skin. Staring, sometimes bloodshot eyes. Blood-red lips; long, sharp canine teeth (which they try to hide from victims until they need them). Some have very long fingernails, like claws. Some vampires wear cloaks.

WHERE THEY LIVE: Many parts of the world, especially Eastern Europe. They are usually found in graves or coffins by day.

POWERS: Strong, fast, can hypnotize people and change into bats, wolves, or even mist.

WEAKNESSES: Repelled by garlic, salt, crucifixes, bright sunlight, running water, holy water, and silver blades. They can be killed by decapitation or by a stake through the heart.

DIET: Blood, blood, and more blood.

OTHER CHARACTERISTICS:
A vampire casts no shadow and can't be seen reflected in a mirror.

FAMOUS VAMPIRES: Serbian peasants Arnold Paole and Peter Plogojowitz, Count Dracula.

VAMPIRES are dead people who have come back to life and feed on the blood of the living. They obtain it by biting people's necks and drinking their blood. If you are bitten by a vampire, unfortunately you will not only die but also become one too. Thankfully, there are several steps you can take to protect yourself.

Above left: The Empusa was a female vampire from Greek mythology that feasted on the blood of men.

ON THE HUNT

Venturing out at night, a vampire can take on the form of a bat or a wolf, or even drift around as a cloud of vapor. Confronting its prey, it hypnotizes the person, bites into their veins, and draws blood until satisfied. The victim feels no pain and later remembers little of the encounter—the only sign may be two puncture marks on the neck made by the vampire's teeth. Gradually, however, the victim will feel woozy and weak and will eventually pass away—only to awake from death a vampire!

NIGHT LOVERS

Vampires are usually the corpses of criminals, suicides, or heretics—people who rejected Christianity. They sleep by day, but at night they rise up and venture forth to quench their thirst for blood.

Most often their daytime resting place is the grave where they were buried. But they can survive in their coffins elsewhere, as long as the coffin contains some soil from their original burial ground. Vampires have also been known to rest in cupboards rather than coffins, hanging upside down like bats. Castles are favored hideouts for vampires, since they are often far away from other houses, good for keeping nosy people out, and full of dark, spooky rooms.

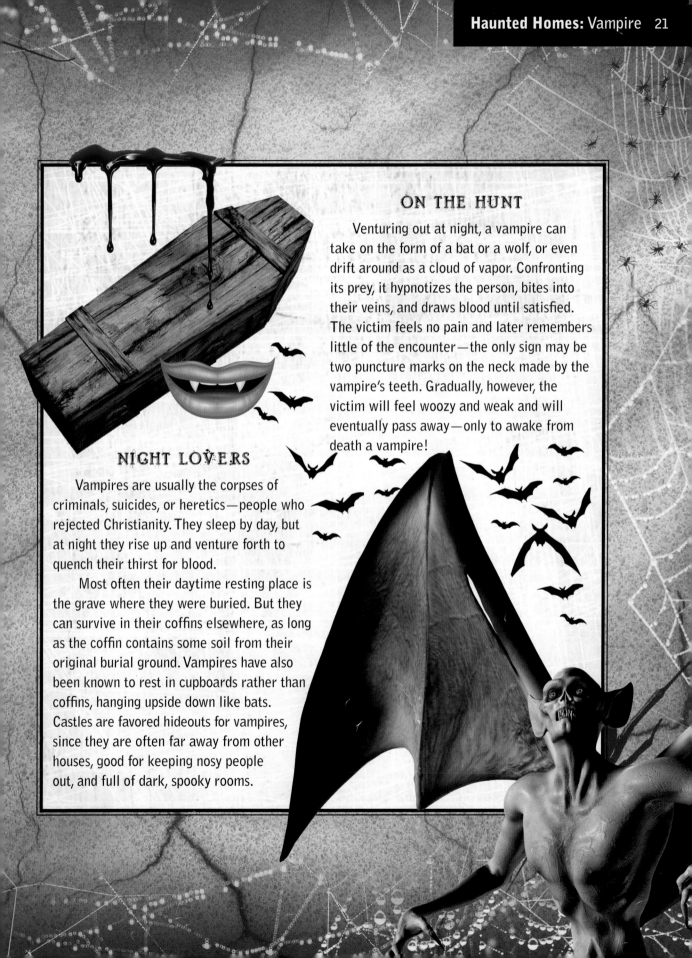

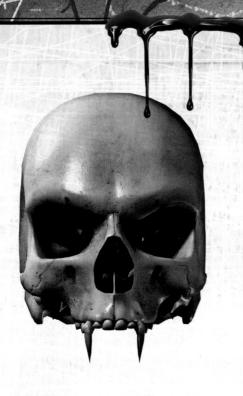

PUBLICITY AND PANIC

From the seventeenth century onwards, belief in vampires was especially strong in the Austro-Hungarian Empire of eastern Europe. Dozens of cases were reported in the early 1700s, including two in rural Serbia —Arnold Paole, who was said to have murdered 16 people after he died, and Peter Plogojowitz, whose resurrected corpse supposedly snacked on and killed several of his neighbors. In both cases (and others), Austrian authorities dug up the body, proclaimed it a true vampire, drove a stake through the heart, and then issued a public report, which of course created widespread panic across Europe for many years.

BLOODSUCKERS

Stories of spirits who feast on the blood of the living have been told around the world for thousands of years. Blood-drinking demons were reported in ancient India, Persia, and Assyria. In Greek mythology, the Empusa is a female monster that sucks the blood out of young men. In Roman myths, the Strix is an owl-like bird that bites humans to obtain blood.

Chinese folklore tells of the Jiang Shi (meaning "stiff corpse"), which hops around on its rigid legs with its arms outstretched and grabs and kills humans to suck out their life essence, or qi. The Penanggalan of Malaysia is a demonic woman whose fanged head separates from her body at night and flies around sucking blood from victims.

Right: Hungarian countess, Elizabeth Báthory.

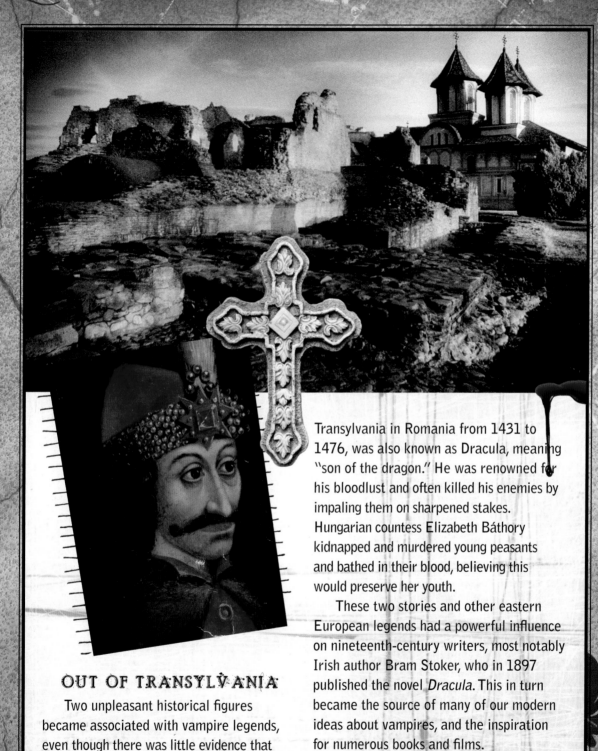

Transylvania in Romania from 1431 to 1476, was also known as Dracula, meaning "son of the dragon." He was renowned for his bloodlust and often killed his enemies by impaling them on sharpened stakes. Hungarian countess Elizabeth Báthory kidnapped and murdered young peasants and bathed in their blood, believing this would preserve her youth.

These two stories and other eastern European legends had a powerful influence on nineteenth-century writers, most notably Irish author Bram Stoker, who in 1897 published the novel *Dracula*. This in turn became the source of many of our modern ideas about vampires, and the inspiration for numerous books and films.

OUT OF TRANSYLVANIA

Two unpleasant historical figures became associated with vampire legends, even though there was little evidence that they had ever bitten anyone in the neck. Vlad Tepes or Vlad the Impaler, ruler of

Above: Vlad the Impaler and his castle.

DRACULA

In Bram Stoker's novel, *Dracula*, Count Dracula lives in a crumbling castle in Transylvania. A visiting Englishman, Jonathan Harker, discovers that the count is a vampire. Managing to escape from the castle, Harker flees to England, but Dracula has his followers transport him there in a coffin and turns one of Harker's friends, Lucy, into a vampire. Soon after, Dracula starts attacking Harker's fiancée, Mina. Dracula runs back to Romania, but Harker follows him and kills him, which is the only way that Mina can be saved.

KEEPING VAMPIRES AT BAY

You're safe from vampires by day, since they will always avoid daylight. Sprinkling salt or holy water along your doorstep and windowsills and hanging a bunch of garlic at the door will prevent a vampire entering your house after dark.

If you have to go out at night, carry garlic with you or, even better, a crucifix— hold it up to a vampire and it will back off quickly. Jumping into or across a river is another way to escape, since vampires loathe running water.

ALL AT STAKE

Getting rid of a vampire for good is tricky, but there are at least a few options. One is to destroy its hiding place and trap it outdoors—it will gradually die if exposed to sunlight, though this could take some time. Another, quicker option is to decapitate it with a gravedigger's spade. But the most popular and proven method is to hammer a sharpened wooden stake—preferably from an elder tree—through the vampire's heart. To make sure the vampire never rises again, you then have to burn the corpse or bury it in a new grave, ideally near a crossroads.

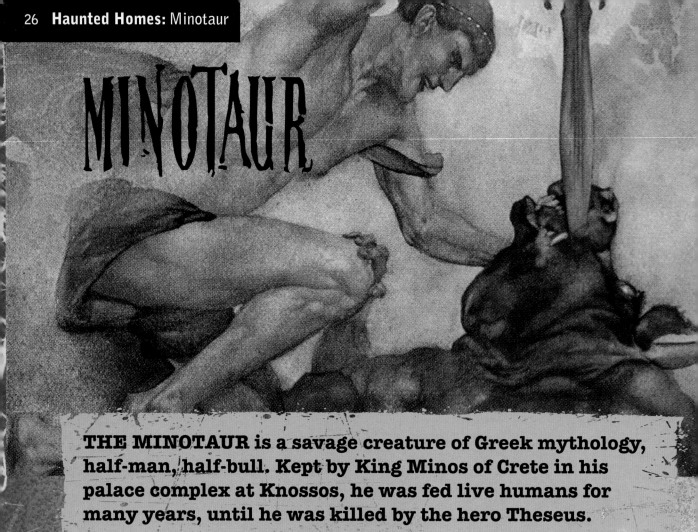

MINOTAUR

THE MINOTAUR is a savage creature of Greek mythology, half-man, half-bull. Kept by King Minos of Crete in his palace complex at Knossos, he was fed live humans for many years, until he was killed by the hero Theseus.

IN THE LABYRINTH

The Minotaur was the monstrous offspring of Minos's wife, Pasiphae, and a white bull sent to Minos by the god Poseidon. To restrain the beast, Minos had it placed at the center of an almost impenetrable labyrinth, or maze. When Minos's son, Androgeos, was killed in Athens, Minos demanded compensation. So, every nine years, the Athenians sent him seven young men and seven young women, and Minos would drive them into the labyrinth to be devoured by the Minotaur.

THESEUS THE HERO

Appalled by the monster, the Athenian warrior Theseus decided he would kill the monster and volunteered to be sent to Knossos as one of the seven young men. When he arrived, Minos's daughter, Ariadne, fell in love with him. Before he entered the labyrinth, she gave him a ball of thread and a sword. Theseus unraveled the thread as he traveled to the center of the labyrinth and, after killing the Minotaur, followed it back to the entrance and escaped from Crete with Ariadne.

FRANKENSTEIN'S MONSTER

Mary Shelley's 1818 novel, *Frankenstein*, describes the creation of one of the most famous storybook monsters.

Swiss scientist Victor Frankenstein decides to make a humanlike creature out of body parts he steals from graveyards. But the creature is so hideous—8 feet (2.5 m) tall with a huge head and ugly yellow skin—that he abandons it. After the monster kills his brother, Frankenstein flees to England then Ireland, but the monster follows him and murders his bride. Desperate to escape, Frankenstein sails to the Arctic, but is pursued by his creation, and both die amid the ice.

RED CAP

If you visit a ruined castle along the border between England and Scotland, watch out for these fearsome goblins.

Red Caps are said to murder travelers and use their blood to dye their hats red, and they must do this often because they perish if their hats dry out or fade. Don't try to flee if you see one, however. For although they look like tiny old men and are weighed down by iron boots, they can run like the wind and have long, talon-like claws to grip and rip. Much better to stand your ground and hold up a crucifix or recite words from the Bible. That sends them scurrying for cover.

GLOSSARY

Apparition: a ghostly figure

Corpse: a dead body

Crucifix: a cross with a figure of Jesus crucified on it

Decapitation: the act of cutting off a head

Fiancée: a woman engaged to be married

Heretic: a person who believes or teaches something opposed to accepted beliefs

Hypnotize: to put someone into a trancelike state

Labyrinth: a maze with complex passageways

Medieval times: the Middle Ages

Medium: a living person who can communicate with the dead

Motif: an idea or theme in a work of art

Mythology: a collection of myths dealing with the gods/goddesses of a particular people

Offspring: the young of a person, animal, or plant

Ouija board: a board with the letters of the alphabet used to communicate with the dead so they can spell out messages

Revenant: one that returns after death

Séance: a meeting of a group of people who try to talk to the dead

Spade: an instrument used for digging

Specter: a ghostly figure

Supernatural: of or relating to an existence beyond the observable universe

Talon: the claw of an animal

Transparent: visible enough to see through

Vapor: gas floating in the air

Wraith: a ghostly figure

INDEX

Please visit our website, www.garethstevens.com. For a free color catalog of all our high-quality books, call toll free 1-800-542-2595 or fax 1-877-542-2596.

Library of Congress Cataloging-in-Publication Data

Cox, Barbara.
Haunted homes / by Barbara Cox and Scott Forbes.
  p. cm. — (Creepy chronicles)
Includes index.
ISBN 978-1-4824-0232-2 (pbk.)
ISBN 978-1-4824-0233-9 (6-pack)
ISBN 978-1-4824-0230-8 (library binding)
1. Haunted houses — Juvenile literature. 2. Supernatural — Juvenile literature. 3. Ghosts — Juvenile literature. 4. Poltergeists—Juvenile literature. I. Title.
BF1461.C69 2014
133.1—dc23

First Edition

Published in 2014 by
Gareth Stevens Publishing
111 East 14th Street, Suite 349
New York, NY 10003

© 2014 Red Lemon Press Limited

Produced for Gareth Stevens by Red Lemon Press Limited
Concept and Project Manager: Ariana Klepac
Designer: Emilia Toia
Design Assistant: Haylee Bruce
Picture Researcher: Ariana Klepac
Text: Scott Forbes (Forest, Castle, Desert), Barbara Cox (all other text)
Indexer: Trevor Matthews

Images: Every effort has been made to trace and contact the copyright holders prior to publication. If notified, the publisher undertakes to rectify any errors or omissions at the earliest opportunity.

Bridgeman Art Library: 2 tl and b, 3 tr, 6 tl and cover, 8 bl in box, 9 b, 10 tr and bl, 11b, 12 t front, 12–13 t (British Library, London), 13 b front (Haags Gemeentemuseum, The Hague, Netherlands), 14 t, 15 tl and br front, 17 t and br in box, 20 tl, 22 br in box, cover and 23 t in box (The Marsden Archive, UK) and bl in box, 24 t, 26 t.
Getty Images: 7 br, 8 tr in box, 9 t, 11 t, 16 br, 18 cl, 19 br in box.
iStockphoto: other images as follows:
cross stitches 6, 8, 9, 11, 18, 19, 23, 27; grunge borders 7, 9, 13, 24; hands 7, 9, 13, 24; mirror 24; stick borders 6, 18, 20; vampire 24; vampire smile 21;
Martin Hargreaves: 16 tl, 27 tl.
Shutterstock: all other images

KEY: t = top, b = bottom, l = left, r = right, c = center

Printed in the United States of America

CPSIA compliance information: Batch #CW14GS: For further information contact Gareth Stevens, New York, New York at 1-800-542-2595.

Gareth Stevens
Publishing